Original title:
Lunar Loops

Copyright © 2025 Creative Arts Management OÜ
All rights reserved.

Author: Rory Fitzgerald
ISBN HARDBACK: 978-1-80567-820-5
ISBN PAPERBACK: 978-1-80567-941-7

## Reveries in the Crescent Light

In the sky, a slice of cheese,
Whispers float with cosmic ease.
Cats on rooftops plot their schemes,
Maybe eat our wildest dreams.

Giggles dance in twilight's glow,
Moonbeams tickle, ebb and flow.
Crickets chirp, they chant a tune,
While owls wink beneath the moon.

## Spheres of Nightly Serenade

A ball of light above our heads,
Makes us sing and dance in beds.
Toadstools jump and stars confide,
In this circus we abide.

Jesters prance with moons in tow,
Drawing laughter, don't you know?
Fireflies join the nightly spree,
Fooling us with their mockery.

## The Pull of Dusk and Dawn

The day fights back with sleepy yawn,
But night plays tricks, and then it's gone.
Bees in dreams buzz like a tune,
While shadows dance beneath the moon.

Caffeine fairies wave hello,
Whirling cups of coffee flow.
Floating high, we laugh and cheer,
As sleepy monsters disappear.

## Craters of Forgotten Tales

Pockmarked beats of past delight,
Echoes from a midnight flight.
Chasing tales on a lunar breeze,
While rabbits munch on cosmic cheese.

Whimsy flows in autumn's dew,
As jester stars wink just for you.
Frogs in bow ties jump and croon,
Sipping tea beneath the moon.

## Cosmic Dances Amidst Stillness

In the shadow of the moon, they pranced,
Chasing stars, the night enhanced.
Aliens slipped and laughed with glee,
Tripping over cosmic debris.

Planets spun like dizzy tops,
Forgetful of their graceful hops.
Asteroids bopped in silly pairs,
While shooting stars lost all their cares.

## **Infinite Circular Motion**

Round and round the Saturn rings,
Dancing cats with feathered wings.
Orbiting in their shiny shoes,
Twirling jigs and silly blues.

Galaxies in goofy flight,
Swaying left and then to the right.
Gravity forgot its solemn job,
As comets spun, a sparkling mob.

## Radiant Whirl

Spinning stories in the dark,
Glistening tales that leave a mark.
Silly moons with faces bright,
Wobbling through the starry night.

With a chuckle, the cosmos sighs,
Making cosmic pizza pies.
Doughy spheres in the vast expanse,
Invite you all to join the dance.

## **Orbiting Heartstrings**

In the embrace of cosmic hugs,
Fluffy clouds and cosmic bugs.
They giggle in the warm embrace,
Bouncing round in silly grace.

Hopping stars with twinkling eyes,
Creating merry little ties.
When comets wink and asteroids tease,
The universe dances with heartstrings' ease.

## The Spiral Path of Dreams.

In the night, the stars collide,
A rabbit hops, it cannot hide.
He wears a hat, so very tall,
And trips on clouds, oh what a fall!

Worms wear ties, to dance and swing,
While crickets chirp, and daisies sing.
Upon this path, we twirl and spin,
Where giggles grow and tickles begin.

## Moonlit Whirls

The moon dons shades, a sight to see,
As owls play cards beneath the tree.
They shuffle light and wink at me,
And giggle like it's all a spree.

Balloons swell up with silly pride,
While fireflies in top hats glide.
They dance and shout in playful bliss,
And twirl till the stars all say, 'What'd we miss!'

## Celestial Echoes

A comet sneezes, fireworks fly,
As penguins waltz beneath the sky.
They slip and slide, then try to leap,
And all the jellybeans just beep!

Wish-granting frogs croak tunes so sweet,
To jive and dance with floppy feet.
Echoing laughs, they spin around,
Creating joy without a sound.

## Dance of the Silver Shadows

Shadows twirl on the floor of night,
One wears socks that are far too tight.
They step on toes and start to sway,
In a bumbling, bouncing ballet play.

Pixies giggle and throw confetti,
As silver beams make lanterns ready.
They flicker bright with zany glee,
While moonbeams dance in jubilee.

## The Whispering Nightfall

The moon giggles bright in the sky,
While stars throw a party, oh my!
They dance on shadows, quite out of tune,
Making wishes on a cheeky balloon.

The owls wear glasses and sip their tea,
Chatting in riddles, wild and free.
The cricket band plays a catchy refrain,
As hedgehogs twirl in a wobbly chain.

## **Eclipsed Wishes**

A shadow played peek-a-boo on the ground,
As silly dreams swirled all around.
Scribbles of starlight crafted a game,
Where wishes giggled, and none were the same.

A cow jumped over the eclipsed delight,
Chasing its tail in the soft moonlight.
With a plop and a splash in a puddle of light,
It belly-flopped into the cobbled night.

## The Eternity of Twilight

In a world where dusk is a playful sprite,
Trying to juggle the stars just right.
Twilight chuckles, it's high on glee,
While clouds wear hats for a spree.

The fireflies wink in a flirty trance,
As shadows trail in a goofy dance.
Then the breeze whispers jokes through the trees,
And giggles explode like poppy seeds.

## **Cascading Celestial Melodies**

The comets whistle a tune of the night,
While planets spin in a dizzy delight.
Galaxies giggle, all twinkly and bright,
Creating symphonies in cosmic bite.

Moons play maracas with clouds all around,
In a concert of chaos where laughter is found.
Stars in tuxedos take to the floor,
While comets race in an encore!

## The Enigma of the Night Sky

In the velvet dusk, the moon's a clown,
Wearing a smile, it floats upside down.
Stars giggle like kids on a sugar high,
Catching glimpses of comet tails in the sky.

A rabbit bounds over on a bicycle bright,
Chasing shadows that flicker with light.
The owls hoot softly, sharing a joke,
As the night drapes its cloak with a poke.

Planets wobble, dance on their toes,
While meteors dive with spectacular shows.
"Hey, look at me!" chirps a shooting star,
As asteroids play catch, not caring where they are.

The night is a carnival, filled with surprise,
Where laughter echoes from the skies.
And while the world sleeps, in slumber so deep,
The cosmos keeps secrets that twinkle and peep.

## Celestial Cradle

In the sky, a bouncing pie,
Round and bright, like a cat that flies,
It giggles down, no reason why,
Chasing stars with silly sighs.

Astronauts dance with rubber boots,
Hopping high in zany suits,
They tickle comets, play kazoo,
And on Mars, they eat green stew.

Space squirrels with acrobatic flair,
Juggle moons without a care,
Floating past in a wobbly chair,
Saying jokes that go nowhere.

With a wink, the sun will peek,
As the planets play hide and seek,
In this cradle of cosmic freaks,
Laughter echoes, making us weak.

## The Enigma of the Night Sphere

A round ball in the sky's embrace,
Winks at folks in a funny chase,
It tells jokes, it loves to tease,
As shadow puppets dance with ease.

Aliens peek through telescopes,
Twirling donuts and dreaming hopes,
With giggles shared in silent screams,
Plotting scripts for cosmic dreams.

The dark gets tickled by a ray,
As craters giggle, wild at play,
While astronauts tripped over their feet,
Landed in a bowl of jelly treat.

Shooting stars with hats so tall,
Tumble down and round we call,
In this sphere, where humor grows,
Space whispers giggles, everyone knows.

## Soft Echoes of the Midnight Echo

A midnight chime in velvet grace,
Wobbling tunes in empty space,
Whispers float with cheeky flair,
Unruly sounds tickle the air.

Rockets dressed in polka dots,
Launch from homes with silly plots,
They zoom past with a chuckled cheer,
Sharing snacks and sipping beer.

Crater critters sing a tune,
Crooning to the lazy moon,
As planets bop with wiggly hips,
While laughter spills from comet tips.

In the echoes of the night,
Giggles bounce, oh what a sight,
Each twinkle brings a smile to share,
As fun unfolds in cosmic air.

## A Moon's Secret Journey

A cheeky moon on a secret flight,
Winks at owls in the dead of night,
It scatters giggles, whispers bright,
Causing shadows to dance with delight.

Tiny stars play tag with glee,
Hiding behind the big pine tree,
While comets wear a silly hat,
Joking with a jumping cat.

Around the earth with tumbles wide,
The moon takes joy in its nightly ride,
Bumping into clouds with a grin,
Creating chaos where it has been.

With a chuckle that echoes clear,
It rolls along, no hint of fear,
On this journey of gleeful jest,
The moon shows us how to have zest.

## Moonlit Whirls

In the sky, a big round face,
Winks at us with such a grace.
Twirling jokes upon the breeze,
Counting stars like quirky fleas.

Crickets giggle, fireflies dance,
While owls plot their midnight prance.
The moon plays tricks, a shining tease,
Hiding sweets among the leaves.

Rabbits hop with socks askew,
Chasing dreams we thought we knew.
What's this? A comet's silly hat?
Oh, what a funny world! Imagine that!

Stars are laughing, making noise,
Whirling round like little boys.
Underneath this silver dome,
The night's a jest we call our home.

## Celestial Spirals

Up above, the moon is sly,
Spinning tales that make us cry.
A cosmic joker in the night,
With glittered jests, it takes flight.

Comets zooming, tripping by,
Twirling like a clumsy fly.
Asteroids join in on the fun,
Dancing 'round, all on the run.

Galaxies twist, a dizzy spree,
Bumping into a cosmic bee.
Planets rolly-polling 'round,
In this circus, laughter's found.

Quasars laugh, and nebulae grin,
As they whirl and spin within.
A universe so full of cheer,
Where clowns of stardust disappear.

## Echoes of the Orb

The orb above, a playful guide,
Whispers stories, laughs collide.
Funny echoes in the void,
Creating joy that can't be toyed.

Frogs serenade beneath its glow,
Telling jokes we'll never know.
Mice debate, "What's cheese, what's moon?"
In this night, we jest and swoon.

With shadows stretching, stretching wide,
They play peek-a-boo, we can't hide.
A rabbit juggles stars with flair,
While the moon rolls back its hair.

Mirthful whispers on the breeze,
Tickle our toes and tease our knees.
In this echo of the night,
Laughter beams, a pure delight.

## The Dance of Shadows

Shadows shimmy on the ground,
Bouncing happily all around.
Moonbeams giggle, silver trails,
As the night spins wild fairy tales.

Cats in hats pirouette with glee,
Dancing near the singing tree.
Owls host parties, whoop and cheer,
Underneath their chandelier.

And what of mice, all dressed in style?
They twirl and spin, oh what a while!
Frolicking with the gentle breeze,
Chasing ducks with mismatched knees.

The moon's a partner, sweet and light,
In this oddball, starry night.
Every shadow, every grin,
Turns the dance into a win!

## **Orbiting Dreams**

In the sky, a silver pie,
That winks at folks passing by.
Jupiter laughs, but oh so sly,
While Saturn spins with rings awry.

Dancing through the night so round,
Gravity pulls, no one's found.
Stars giggle, making a sound,
As silly shadows swirl around.

## The Night's Spiral Serenade

Balloons float in cosmic fun,
Chasing comets, one by one.
The moon hums a tune on the run,
While aliens giggle, quite a ton.

With candy stars that twinkle bright,
They play tag in galactic light.
Planets join in, such a sight,
In the merry dance of night.

## Phases of a Whisper

A full moon grins with a cheeky shine,
While wobbly stars mix in the wine.
Whispers come with a twist of vine,
As meteors plot a prank divine.

Eclipses giggle, wearing shades,
Light plays hide and seek in raids.
They spin around in funny parades,
Making memories that never fade.

## Tides of Reflection

Waves splash with a sloshing cheer,
The ocean laughs, can you hear?
Moonbeams dance without a fear,
As fish throw parties, oh so clear.

Life's a ripple, a goofy race,
Water spirits join the chase.
In this bubbly, jolly space,
Together they celebrate their place.

## Time's Celestial Waltz

The clock danced on the wall, so spry,
With hands that waved like a butterfly.
Tick-tock went the ears of the cat,
Chasing shadows, just imagine that!

As time spun round, the stars wore gowns,
Each planet grinned, as if to clown.
Moments slipped like soap from hands,
The moon teased tides with silly bands!

## **The Hedged Glow**

A hedgehog glowed beneath the moons,
Playing hide and seek with silver spoons.
He rolled in curves, a prickly ball,
Polka dots made him quite the thrall!

The garden laughed with every breeze,
As veggies danced, with grace and ease.
Carrots twirled and onions spun,
In this odd ball, who needs the sun?

## Enfolded in Night's Charm

The night wore a cloak of twinkling jokes,
With giggles shared by million strokes.
The bats played tag, a sky-born game,
While owls hooted, calling their name.

A comet zipped by, all dressed up,
Stirring cosmic gossip in a cup.
Stars winked slyly, mischievous and bright,
As dreams pranced around in sheer delight!

## **The Silver Thread of Time**

Time spun a thread so shiny and thin,
It tangled the kittens with every spin.
They leaped and bounced in a fluffy quest,
While giggles echoed from east to west.

The moon rolled over, with a chuckle so loud,
"Let's party on rooftops, gather the crowd!"
As seconds slipped by in a silly race,
Each moment was grinning, full of embrace!

## Gaze of the Radiant Sphere

When the moon takes a peek, oh what a sight,
It winks at the world, dancing in the night.
Cats strut like stars, they think they're so sly,
While dogs bark at shadows, thinking they fly.

Telescope pointed, I squint at the beam,
Where astronauts lived, or so goes the dream.
Eating cheese with my tongue, I'm ready to dive,
For cosmic fondue is how I feel alive!

## Tides of the Hidden Glow

The ocean waves giggle, they rise and they fall,
Chasing moonbeams like children, they heed the call.
Seashells are laughing, tickled by the tide,
As starfish do somersaults, all open wide.

Crabs host a party, dancing on the shore,
While seagulls provide the tunes, begging for more.
A jellyfish limbo, just swaying, so free,
In this beach bash, who needs gravity?

**Chasing Light Across the Sky**

I've got my sneakers, it's time to take flight,
Chasing twinkling stars, oh what a delight!
Jumping on rooftops, with friends, we will twirl,
Underneath the sky, we spin and we whirl.

The moon starts to giggle, it knows we are near,
A dance party's brewing, can you hear the cheer?
With marshmallow fluff, we toast on a stick,
Starlit adventures, let's pick up the pace quick!

## The Cycle of Selenic Shadows

Shadows are waltzing, under twilight's embrace,
While the moon plays the clown, with a grin on its face.
Whiskers are twitching, as critters creep by,
In the game of hide and seek, who can deny?

Batty bats flutter, in hats they do sip,
Caught up in a whirl, they lose their grip.
With laughter and giggles, they whirl on their way,
In the glimmering glow, they play and they sway.

## The Cosmic Spiral

In the night sky, a rubber band,
Stretching far, oh what a plan!
Bouncing stars, they do collide,
In this dance, we take a ride.

Planets pirouetting with glee,
Wobbling like a tipsy bee.
Galaxies laugh, they swirl around,
Gravity's clown, a joyful sound.

Twinkling lights make silly faces,
Chasing dreams in galactic races.
Asteroids juggle, meteors joke,
In this scheme, the cosmos pokes.

Round and round, they tango through,
Sky's a stage for the cosmic crew.
With a wink and a cheeky grin,
Another loop, let's spin again!

## Harmony of the Glowing Orb

A ball of cheese, oh what a sight,
Dancing mice in the moonlight.
With every bounce, they squeak and slide,
In dreams of snacks, they joyfully glide.

The shadows play a game of tag,
While stars wear hats, that's quite a brag!
The craters giggle in sweet delight,
Under the glow of the frosty night.

Rabbits race on lunar lanes,
In rocket shoes, they feel no pains.
As comets trail with icy spritz,
The cosmic show, it never quits!

Oh floating orb, you jest and tease,
As laughter fills the evening breeze.
In this ballet, let's take a chance,
With moonlit joys, let's twirl and dance!

## Navigating Through Night's Song

A sailor on a ship of beams,
Navigates through silly dreams.
With a compass made of jelly beans,
He laughs aloud, or so it seems.

Stars are guides in this quirky ride,
With giggles echoing far and wide.
The waves are whispers, oh so light,
In this fun trip through the night.

Neptune's pranks make the sailors shout,
Dancing waves, there's never doubt.
Hearts are full of rhythm's cheer,
As silly crabs twist in the rear.

With each moonbeam, we sing along,
In the laughter of the night's song.
Navigating with joy, we steer,
On this wild trip, we have no fear!

## Celestial Pathways

Oh comet tail, so bright and bold,
Draws a map of stories told.
On stardust paths we take a stroll,
Giggles wrap us like a scroll.

Meteor showers rain down glee,
Splashing colors for all to see.
Space raccoons dance 'neath the beams,
Chasing dreams in silver streams.

Bigfoot swings from Saturn's rings,
While aliens hum and dance with flings.
Each step we take, a bouncing cheer,
In the cosmic carnival, we persevere.

As the universe claps and sways,
Come join the fun in the starry maze!
In these celestial and funny ways,
We'll celebrate the cosmic craze!

## **Rhythms of the Fading Glow**

The moon forgot its dance today,
Tripped on stars, fell in a sway.
It giggled while it brushed its face,
And spun around in silly grace.

The craters laughed, they knew the tune,
While comets tooted like a loon.
Each beam a joke, a playful jest,
As night wore on, it just confessed.

With shadows cast in funky shapes,
The night just grinned and made mistakes.
A cosmic giggle, all around,
As orbs of silver twirled and bound.

So here we are, at midnight's play,
Admiring how the planets sway.
In laughter's grip, we find our place,
A dreamy waltz, a smiling space.

## A Serenade in Circular Decay

In circles round, the saturnine,
Sings high, then low, a comical line.
It caught a comet, called it Stan,
Together they devised a plan.

The stars snickered, brave and bold,
As orbits twisted, tales retold.
Falling planets, laughing too,
Chasing after a jelly moon.

With each bright flash, a wink will dart,
The universe is quite the art.
A serenade rich with forgets,
As gravity plays its silly bets.

So dance away with whims at night,
Comets frolic in pure delight.
It's just a phase, don't take it tough,
The cosmos laughs, it's never rough.

# Refracted in the Midnight Air

A glow misplaced, the sprites all cheer,
Bouncing off planets, far and near.
They hop and skip on silver beams,
And juggle laughter in moonlit dreams.

The satellites spark and twirl in space,
Tickled by time, they leave no trace.
While asteroids wear a silly hat,
And swap strange stories with a bat.

Through refracted light, a sight to see,
A party forming, wild and free.
With constellations doing the twist,
No night's complete without this list.

In midnight's air, a joyful dance,
Engaging hearts in cosmic chance.
So join the fun, don't miss the show,
Where mirth and stars forever glow.

## **Enigmas of the Night's Embrace**

The twilight whispers, secrets spun,
In riddles wrapped, a game begun.
With moons that puff and stars that wink,
The cosmos chuckles, quick as a blink.

A spacecraft lost, it roams the wild,
With Martians drawing doodles, mild.
The night enfolds with playful grace,
As chaos soars in sweet embrace.

A giggle from a distant sun,
Sparks all the mischief just for fun.
The planets spin in laughter's fold,
Unraveling stories yet untold.

In every quirk, a story thrives,
In mysteries where the joy arrives.
So dance along, don't miss the chase,
In enigmas where the night finds space.

## **Moonbeams in Circles**

Round and round, the beams do play,
Chasing shadows night and day.
A game of tag with the stars above,
Whispering secrets, oh what a love.

Winking quickly, they dance with glee,
Mischief hides in every spree.
The moon forgot where it should land,
Oh, where's that bright but silly hand?

A giggle here, a sparkle there,
The night's a joker, full of flair.
Catch me if you can, they tease,
While rustling through the nighttime breeze.

It's a bouncy ball of shining light,
Juggling dreams in the cool night.
Those beams can't sit and stay, you see,
Who knew the moon could be so free?

## Celestial Ribbons

Tangled strands of shimmering thread,
Across the sky, they joyfully spread.
Twist and twirl in a cosmic race,
A ribbon dance in the starry space.

With colors bright, they swirl around,
Each twist and turn, a giggling sound.
Oh, what's this? A knot they make,
The universe laughs; it's a silly mistake!

Hitching rides on a comet's tail,
These ribbons soar, they never fail.
Wrapping planets in tight embrace,
A cosmic hug in a playful chase.

At every turn, they play their game,
In the sky, there's no one to tame.
If you trip over one, don't you fret,
It's just a loop; no need to regret!

## The Roundabout of Night

Here we go, a spin so sly,
Roundabout in the velvet sky.
With every turn, a star will blink,
Dizzy dreams pour in like ink.

Twist and twirl, hang on tight,
Grab a friend for extra flight.
Laughter echoes, 'round we go,
Can't stop now; it's the show!

The moon shouts, 'Hey, watch your step!'
As stardust rains, they take the rep.
Around and round, we lose our way,
But in the fun, who wants to stay?

Silly loops that tickle the core,
Scrambling laughter, we want more.
On this ride, all worries melt,
In this roundabout, pure joy is felt.

## Echoes of Celestial Motion

In the night's embrace, echoes sing,
A choir of chaos, what joy they bring!
Under the stars, so wild and free,
The universe giggles at you and me.

With a bounce, a bounce, off they go,
Chasing comets, stealing the show.
Echoes ricochet, laughter flows,
Among the moons, who really knows?

In dizzy spirals, shadows play,
A cosmic circus, come what may.
Juggling worlds with moonlit pride,
As meteors wink and take a ride.

Oh dear moon, won't you stay awhile?
With twinkling tales to make us smile.
Echoes of motion, what a delight,
In this funny dance of the starry night!

## Veils of Silver Light

In shadows, knees bend low,
The moon winks with a glow.
Cats in hats dance around,
Laughing at stars that tumble down.

A squirrel dons a shining cape,
Dares the rabbit to escape.
Crickets hide, a jig they choose,
While owls drop their dreams in blues.

With cheese on sticks, the mice all feast,
As fireflies bumble, to say the least.
A giggle erupts from the bushy trees,
Nature's party, an endless tease.

So sip some dew, join the fun,
The night is young; there's room for one.
With laughter echoing all around,
In veils of silver, joy is found.

# The Ballet of the Night Glow

In tutus bright, the stars pirouette,
With winks and twirls, a cosmic bet.
Balloons of air made of soft light,
Bounce around in silly flight.

A raccoon joins with a bow on top,
Clumsily bouncing, he cannot stop.
With a jive here and a twirl there,
Each clap and stomp fills the air.

The owls hoot a funky beat,
While shadows swift pick dancing feet.
In this grand show, all critters play,
The forest giggles, hip-hip-hooray!

As the night fades, and curtains close,
They tip their hats, in playful prose.
Under the glow, they dance with glee,
In the ballet, wild and free.

## Flickers in the Celestial Dance

Stars take turns, a glimmery spin,
Flickers around, let the fun begin.
Planetary pals join for a race,
Jupiter rolling with grace and pace.

While comets pass, they play tag,
Galaxies whirl with a playful brag.
Asteroids hop with clattering sounds,
As laughter echoes through space's bounds.

A giggle erupts from the Milky Way,
As meteors zoom, they glide and sway.
The universe revels, wild and bold,
In sparkling antics that never get old.

With stardust confetti in every nook,
Cosmic surprises on every hook.
Flickers and fun in celestial prance,
Join the party, join the dance!

# Rhythms of the Enchanted Night

As shadows stretch and moonbeams play,
Sound of chuckles fills the bay.
Those little elves with bells and glee,
Hop on mushrooms as merry as can be.

With clapping hooves and whiskered grins,
Tiny toadstools join in spins.
A mischievous breeze whispers bright,
Leading all in the dance of the night.

Squirrels race up bright stars so clear,
Juggling acorns, full of cheer.
The night sky rumbles with giggly sighs,
Under the watch of winked-out eyes.

In enchanted rhythms, every heart beats,
With shadows waltzing to magical feats.
Join the fiesta, stay for the light,
In the rhythms of the wondrous night.

## Celestial Following

In the night, I dance and prance,
The moonlight leads a silly chance.
Stars giggle, winking bright,
As I chase them with delight.

A comet zooms, I shout with glee,
"Catch me, catch me!" says the spree.
But it's too fast, it takes a spin,
Laughing at the chase I'm in.

Satellites hide, they play peekaboo,
They throw moon pies, just for you!
I trip and tumble, a cosmic race,
With a grin plastered on my face.

So here's to nights with playful charms,
Where starlight tickles and moonlight warms.
I follow paths where laughter glows,
In this celestial game, anything goes!

## Wandering with the Moonlight

Oh, wandering light that skips and hops,
You lead me where the fun never stops.
With shadows playing tag behind,
And giggles echoing in my mind.

The trees make faces, a leafy crew,
As I waltz beneath your silver hue.
Crickets chirp a silly tune,
I can't help but jiggle with the moon.

I find a puddle that reflects my grin,
A moonlit disco, let the party begin!
I moonwalk through the glimmering night,
With twinkling stars as my spotlight.

So let's frolic till the break of day,
With whimsical shades that sway and play.
A caper beneath this charming glow,
Together we'll steal the evening show!

## Shadows of a Silent Journey

In shadows deep, I tiptoe along,
The night hums a funny song.
With giggles trapped in the northern breeze,
I'm on a mission, if you please.

My shadow waves, it flirts and flops,
It keeps me company, never stops.
Chasing fireflies like a curious sprite,
We prank the moon till the morning light.

Up above, constellations play,
They throw down wishes and jokes all day.
I catch one, it whispers in my ear,
"Don't take life too seriously, dear!"

So I dance with shadows, full of cheer,
In this silent journey, there's nothing to fear.
Laughter echoes, here and there,
With twinkling stars, we're quite the pair!

## A Cycle of Dreaming

Round and round like a carousel,
Dreams spin wildly, can't you tell?
The moon beams down a silver grin,
Inviting dreams to dance and spin.

I hop on clouds, soft as cream,
Where giggles bubble, a perfect dream.
With every twirl and every twist,
I find a moment I've missed.

Time is slippery like soap, you see,
In this playful realm, we're all so free.
I ride a star, what a funny ride,
Giggling with space on this cosmic slide.

So let's embrace this silly game,
In a cycle of dreaming, nothing's the same.
With laughter lighting the endless night,
We'll twirl forever, a delightful sight!

## **Circulating Starlight**

In the sky, a dance of glee,
Stars spinning wildly, can't you see?
A cosmic joke, a glittering chase,
Planets bumping in a cheeky race.

The sun is giggling, what a sight,
Chasing shadows through the night.
Comets make a snack of clouds,
While constellations laugh out loud.

Winking twinklers, doing flips,
Astronauts tossing cosmic chips.
Cosmic hiccups, gravity's tease,
Galaxies swirling with the greatest ease.

Moonbeams stretch in silly poses,
Tickling stardust and falling roses.
Orbiting dreams and lighthearted schemes,
Crafted in the universe's wildest dreams.

## **The Mirage of the Moon**

A silver orb with a cheeky grin,
Hiding behind clouds, let the games begin!
What's that? An owl sharing a snack?
Oh wait, it's just a squirrel, dressed in black.

Moonlight pranks on sleepy towns,
Chasing cats while wearing crowns.
The shadows giggle, playing chess,
While stardust gives them an elegant dress.

The nightingale joins in on the jest,
Singing silly rhymes, doing its best.
Elves in pajamas, a dance they share,
As the moon chuckles, swinging in the air.

Echoes of laughter weaving through the night,
Illusions of bubbles, floating in flight.
The moon spins tales of fun and cheer,
Serenading the stars with a winking leer.

## **Twilight's Spiraled Song**

Twilight arrives, the stage is set,
With colors swirling, a splendid bet.
Fireflies giggle, twinkling bright,
While crickets crank up their evening flight.

The sun and stars trade silly jokes,
As dreamers gather in cozy cloaks.
Frogs croak rhythms, dancing feet,
While moonbeams join in for a sweet treat.

Rabbits in bow ties, all on parade,
Delivering dreams in a sonic serenade.
Songs of the evening, playful and light,
As the world turns on, oh what a sight!

Laughing shadows, don't be shy,
Join the merry twinkle in the sky.
Twilight's symphony echoes so long,
In the heart of night, we'll sing along.

## Observations Under a Celestial Dome

Beneath the sky, a curious crew,
With telescopes aiming, oh what a view!
Aliens playing hopscotch on Mars,
Giggles and gasps from the land of stars.

Asteroids tossing confetti in space,
Meteor showers, a celestial race.
Cosmic clowns juggling light with flair,
While Saturn shows off its fluffy hair.

Stars are gossiping, they can't keep still,
Under the dome, there's laughter to spill.
Nebulae dance in puffs of pink,
And comets slide by with a wink.

Each twinkle holds a puzzling riddle,
While constellations play on their fiddle.
Observing the merriment above,
In celestial chaos, we find our love.

## Night's Enchanted Swirls

In shadows where the moonlight plays,
A cat in boots leads silly ways.
With twirls and twists, it does a jig,
While stars chuckle, oh so big.

The wind gives chase, a playful race,
While owls hoot, keeping pace.
The night winks back with a sly smile,
Come join the fun, just for a while.

With bouncing foxes and dancing larks,
They spin around like glowing sparks.
A party hosted by the night,
Where dreams take flight with pure delight.

So grab your cloak and join the spree,
In this swirling world of glee!
For laughter echoes through the skies,
As moonbeams dance and mischief flies.

## **Waves of Silver Dreams**

A whale of dreams swims in the sea,
With jellyfish that giggle with glee.
They surf on waves both big and small,
Chasing bubbles as they rise and fall.

The crabber crabs with giant claws,
Hilarious poses, just because!
Starfish join in, a wiggly crew,
With a ticklish touch that's all too true.

The shoreline's echo, a laugh-filled tone,
Seagulls crack jokes when they moan.
Their feathery friends flip and fly,
As if in jest, they kiss the sky.

So ride the tides, let laughter bloom,
In silver dreams that spell out 'Zoom!'
You'll find that joy within the sea,
A playful splash for you and me!

## Reflections in Starlit Glass

A mirror realm where wishes gleam,
Where nothing's ever as it seems.
A frog in specs checks its hair,
Then leaps to dance without a care.

The moon spills secrets to the trees,
While squirrels giggle in the breeze.
With bottles twinkling, tales unfurl,
As fireflies weave a glowing whirl.

The owls play cards, a game of chance,
While frogs pull off a dapper dance.
The stars ignite with cheeky spells,
Their laughter ringing like small bells.

So twirl and spin in this bright glass,
Where silliness is sure to amass.
For in this world of laugh and sigh,
Reflections shine as spirits fly.

## The Orbit of Whispers

In circles round, the whispers glide,
With giggles bouncing, side by side.
A rabbit with a quirk, oh dear,
Knows every secret here—don't fear!

The comet trails a funny face,
As laughter echoes through the space.
A dance of shadows, silly prance,
While stars applaud this cosmic dance.

Asteroids roll with a chuckle loud,
While Saturn's rings wear a rainbow shroud.
And moons that wink like mischief's kin,
Are grinning wide—let the fun begin!

So stay a while and spin with ease,
In this orbit where laughter frees.
For whispers twirl, both soft and bright,
Creating joy that fills the night.

## Embrace of the Midnight Tide

Under the stars, a squirrel pranced,
Wearing shades, he too had danced.
The moon, it winked with glee and chatter,
As jellyfish swam, their disco platter.

A crab wore pants, oh so very bright,
Claiming he'd win the costume night.
But slippery fish, in sequins they twirled,
In this odd realm, all senses whirled.

Dolphins joked, 'We're the real stars!'
While seaweed waved, 'You can't park cars!'
With bubbles popping, the night grew louder,
In this midnight tide, nothing felt prouder.

So raise your fins, and wave your claws,
Join the laugh, for what's the cause?
In the embrace of tides so wide,
Life's a laugh on this joyful ride.

# Dreams in a Moonbeam

A cat in pajamas, snoozing so deep,
Chased by moonbeams, he starts to leap.
With cheese-shaped dreams, he runs and slides,
Through fields of cream where no one hides.

Gummy bears dance on marshmallow fluff,
'This is the life!' they squeal, 'So tough!'
But a chocolate river flows close by,
With a wink, it whispers, 'Give it a try!'

Puppies in hats, oh what a sight,
Sipping on cocoa, feeling just right.
While clouds wear socks, fluffy and bright,
In this moonbeam realm, all feels light.

So gather your dreams, bring your cheer,
In this land of whimsy, there's nothing to fear!
For each sweet vision leads us astray,
In dreams lit by beams, we'll laugh all day.

## **The Gravity of Nightfall**

At nighttime picnics, ants take the prize,
Dragging crumbs beneath starry skies.
A raccoon stole a sandwich, so bold,
Proclaiming, 'This feast is pure gold!'

A bear wore boots, strutting with flair,
Stepping on leaves without a care.
The fireflies said, 'Don't lose the beat!'
As hedgehogs lined up for a dance on their feet.

Bathtubs floating in puddles of glue,
Pigs in space suits, what a silly view!
Each star overhead was chuckling light,
As laughter echoed through the crisp night.

With gravity lost, we'll twirl and spin,
This is our time, let the fun begin!
So join the frolic, in joy we'll enthrall,
For in the dark, we're having a ball.

## Whispers from the Sky

Clouds share secrets, giggly and loud,
While raindrops form a chuckling crowd.
A penguin swung by, on a kite made of zest,
Said, 'Flying's the best, much better than rest!'

Stars gave high fives, all glitter and shine,
While comets zoomed past, their laughter in line.
One wished for pizza, the other for cake,
Said, 'Let's dine together for laughter's sake!'

Moonbeams tickled the trees in their way,
While owls hooted jokes, 'It's a hoot every day!'
Kittens on scooters dashed left and right,
In this sky of whispers, all felt so light.

So join the chatter, the giggles and cheer,
For in skies so silly, we forget all our fear.
In whispers from above, joy forever flies,
In a world of laughter that never denies.

## **The Gentle Pull of Night**

The moon winks in a quiet jest,
Tugging at tides like a fun-loving guest.
Stars giggle as they twinkle bright,
Playing hide and seek all night.

Crickets chirp a melodious tune,
While owls wear monocles under the moon.
They debate on who's the best dressed,
In shadows of night, they jest and jest!

A comet zooms by, a cheeky surprise,
Leaving trails of sparkles in the skies.
The night sways as laughter blends,
In this cosmic dance, joy never ends.

So let's twirl with the stars' bright gleam,
In the funny ballet of night's sweet dream.
With each giggle, a tale to spin,
Under the charm where chuckles begin.

## **Between the Stars' Embrace**

In velvet blue, the stars have fun,
Moonbeam limousines for everyone.
They race through the skies, what's the plan?
To prank the sun, if they can!

A comet's tail, a glittering tease,
Gathers a crowd, makes wishes with ease.
"Catch me if you can!" they all scream,
As the galaxy giggles, or so it seems.

Nebulae gather for a starry ball,
With planetary pastries, oh, they enthrall.
Meteor showers rain confetti bright,
In the space dance party of the night.

With one last twist, the universe grins,
As the orbiting giggles remind us of wins.
In this cosmic comedy, don't be shy,
Let's laugh with the stars and reach for the sky!

## Timing the Moon's Breath

Moonbeams stretch on a lazy spree,
Yawning clouds play hide and seek glee.
The lunar clock ticks, soft and slow,
In rhythms of laughter, joy's sweet flow.

Each silver sigh sends ripples away,
Tickling the comets that join in the play.
The night's whispers hold prompts to embrace,
As dreams pirouette through cosmic space.

Stars try to keep time with a silly dance,
Wobbling around in a twinkling trance.
Galaxies chuckle in swirling delight,
In teasing the shadows that creep in the night.

So count the giggles, just follow the beat,
In this cosmic rhythm, the night feels sweet.
Through each soft tick of the moon's gentle breath,
Let's join the secrets of laughter and jest!

# Roundabout Reflections

The moons spin round like a merry-go,
Making faces at stars down below.
Planets join in, a cosmic charade,
As the universe giggles in glittering parade.

Eclipses play peek-a-boo, oh what fun!
Shadows dance lightly, making us run.
In the mirror of space, all is a bloom,
Reflecting bright laughs in the night's room.

Asteroids bounce with a bump and a spin,
Tickling each comet, inviting them in.
Nebula's yarns weave stories so grand,
Creating a tapestry, we cannot understand!

With each twirling star, let us embrace,
The joyous chaos of this vast space.
As we whirl through the night, hearts full of cheer,
Roundabout reflections keep laughter near.

## **Orbital Reverie**

A cow jumped high, a starry flight,
In pajamas, moonlit sight.
Chasing whispers, giggles bright,
Around the world, what a night!

Socks and sandals, fashion trend,
A comet trails, oh, my dear friend.
With silly games that never end,
We'll laugh and twirl, round the bend.

Noses up, catching light,
Floating in a cosmic kite.
Grapes and cheese, a tasty bite,
Waving hello to satellite!

Dancing shadows play a tune,
Mickey Mouse with a bright balloon.
Follow that wiggly raccoon,
As we glide to the laughing moon!

## Shadows in the Twilight Spiral

Balloons and bubbles float on by,
A snail has dreams of learning to fly.
Wobbling over, touching the sky,
Where sock puppets nibble on pie!

Stars wear hats, a silly sight,
While jellybeans twinkle in delight.
The funny fish swims left and right,
Chasing dreams all through the night.

A gopher sings in goofy tones,
While bicycles dance on their bones.
Twilight whispers funny puns,
As the disco moon plays for fun!

Glitter balls that bounce and spin,
A cheery owl grins with a grin.
Shadow games with a mischievous grin,
Twilight's giggle draws us in!

## The Enchanted Crescent


A banana boat sails the bright stream,
With marshmallow clouds and candy cream.
Glowing flowers that giggle and beam,
In the sparkle of a daydream.

Bouncing donuts run a race,
While ice cream castles fill the space.
A sneaky cat with a silly face,
Pursues his tail in endless chase.

Puppies dance in a sparkling hat,
Beneath a shimmering acrobat.
Juggling stars and a chatty bat,
Props for a show—the cosmic spat!

As the night gets ready to swoon,
The jester sings to the giggling moon.
Everyone smiles—who'll be marooned?
In this magical, jolly tune!

# **Reflection in Orbit**

A mirror ball spins with flair,
While pancakes float without a care.
Jelly jars dance in the air,
As unicorns wiggle in laughter there.

Peanut butter glues the clouds,
As rubber ducks swim in proud shrouds.
A wiggly worm in giggly crowds,
Dancing wildly, shouting loud!

Floating bicycles bounce on beams,
While gummy bears share quirky dreams.
In this fun, sparkling seam,
We pop and giggle like moonlit streams!

Rockets built from shiny pies,
Soar with laughter toward the skies.
With each giggle, the evening flies,
In our world of fun—no goodbyes!

## **The Bright Loop of Midnight**

The moon danced high, so full of glee,
It tripped on clouds, a sight to see.
With cheeky grins, it spun around,
And coaxed the night with silly sounds.

Stars twinkled back, so bright and bold,
They whispered jokes that never grow old.
The crickets chimed in, a cheerful band,
While owls hooted laughs, perfectly planned.

A comet zipped by, with a wink and a nod,
Chasing a firefly, who played the fool's prod.
Each twist and turn brought giggles galore,
As laughter soared high, who could ask for more?

The night wore on with laughter's embrace,
The moon kept tumbling, a silly race.
As dawn drew near, the chuckles would fade,
Yet memories lingered, a joyous parade.

## Silvered Paths of Elysium

Up in the sky, the moon wore a hat,
Made of cheese, how silly is that?
It slid down the beams, like a kid on a slide,
While stars cheered it on, bursting with pride.

A rabbit with wings hopped over the scene,
Carrying carrots, all bright and green.
They flipped through the air, in ridiculous loops,
Chasing each other, like giggling troops.

Jupiter cracked jokes, amidst distant rings,
While Venus sang songs about fanciful things.
The galaxy chuckled, an endless delight,
As cosmic creatures joined in the night.

Each twinkling spark had a story to tell,
Of laughter and pranks, oh wouldn't it sell?
These silvered paths of whimsy and fun,
Under the watch of the grinning sun.

## **Constellations in Motion**

Dancing, the stars put on quite a show,
With rhythmic twirls and a luminous flow.
They formed into shapes, all quirky and bright,
While giggles erupted at their silly sight.

The Big Dipper slid, then took a quick leap,
Splashing the Milky Way, bringing starlight to weep.
And Cassiopeia, with her dramatic flair,
Tossed popcorn across the celestial air.

A unicorn comet raced past in a flash,
With a tail made of candy and stars that do splash.
They played tag with meteors, both fast and so spry,
Chasing each other, just zooming on high.

With laughter and sass, the cosmos did sway,
As constellations giggled the night into day.
Their playful ballet, a sight to behold,
In the canvas of darkness, where dreams could unfold.

## **Gentle Radiance Unwound**

The moon wore slippers, soft as a dream,
As it pranced through the night, like a starry stream.
With a wink at the Earth, it began to tease,
A gentle radiance that aimed to please.

Fireflies chuckled, with a dance of delight,
As shadows played tag in the warm summer's night.
The trees started rustling, pretending to nap,
While rustling leaves sent down a gentle clap.

A parade of dreams, all whimsical jest,
With giggling wishes that simply won't rest.
The soft glow of night, like a child's sweet laugh,
Spun stories of joy, their beautiful craft.

So let the moon glide, with its soft, silly grace,
As we sway to the rhythm of this starry race.
In the gentle radiance, laughter is found,
In the night's sweet embrace, let joy be unbound.

## Orbiting Odysseys

In circles we twirl, like a cat on a rug,
Chasing shadows and shoes, oh what a tug!
We spin and we giggle, in this grand parade,
Who knew gravity felt like a lighthearted charade?

With each silly loop, we reach for the sky,
Pretending to fly as we both tumble by.
The ground catches us, with a soft friendly thud,
Oh, to dance in the cosmos, with laughter and mud!

Around and around, we play hide and seek,
Behind the bright stars, we peek and we squeak.
A tug on a comet, a pull from the breeze,
Cartwheels through stardust, oh what a tease!

So let's orbit forever, with joy in our hearts,
In these zany adventures, no one departs.
With telescope giggles, and moonbeam delight,
We'll ride on our rockets, through the endless night!

## The Ellipse of Affection

Our love is an orbit, oh isn't it grand?
We loop-de-loop 'round, hand in hand.
Around the big cheese, we giggle and spin,
Two silly astronauts, where to begin?

You stole my heart with a comet's bright tail,
A wink and a nudge, we set off to sail.
We gather up stardust, in mismatched space suits,
Trading barbs like meteors, oh how it zoots!

Each time we collide, it's not on the nose,
But rather a hug, and a tickle, and who knows?
We twirl in our ellipse, with laughter so free,
Bouncing to rhythms of cosmic glee.

With joy in our orbits, we wave to the rest,
As we gather our moons, we feel truly blessed.
In this funny old galaxy, our hearts are the same,
Two quirky adventurers, playing love's game!

## **Embraced by Starry Trails**

Through trails of bright sparkles, we play and we drift,
With showers of giggles, the universe is our gift.
In our cosmic embrace, we share silly stunts,
Like in a grand circus, under starlit fronts.

From planets to moons, we dance and we sway,
A wobbly waltz on this sidereal play.
We twirl 'til we tumble, and share cosmic pies,
Flung from a comet, oh how time flies!

With each playful plummet and jovial grab,
We knit our own tapestry, a celestial fab!
Trading starry secrets with whispers and grins,
Like bubbles of laughter, our frolic begins.

In the embrace of the night, we make goofy fates,
With stardust confetti and starry crates.
Two partners in space, finding joy is our art,
As we whirl through the cosmos, forever, sweetheart!

**Phases of the Night**

Oh, look at us now, in our phases of play,
We're giddy as moons, in a bright ballet!
From crescent to full, our giggles expand,
As we leap and we bound, hand in hand.

The night plays a joke, with shadows that dance,
Twisting and turning, we take our chance.
With each new encounter, our laughter takes flight,
Like fireflies prancing in the cloak of the night.

We slip and we slide like a pair of comets,
Wearing silly hats, oh we're quite the muses!
With jokes made of starlight, and whispers of glee,
In the phases we share, you're the moon next to me.

So let's bask in the glow of this nightly parade,
With giggles like stardust, and friendships remade.
In the phases of night, we'll spin with delight,
Two dreamers adrift in the thrill of the night!

www.ingramcontent.com/pod-product-compliance
Lightning Source LLC
Chambersburg PA
CBHW071834160426
43209CB00003B/301